STOCK CAR LEGENDS

STOCK CAR LEGENDS:

The Laughs, Practical Jokes, and Fun Stories
From
Racing's Greats!

By Ronda Jackson Martin

PREMIUM PRESS AMERICA
NASHVILLE, TENNESSEE

STOCK CAR LEGENDS: The Laughs, Practical Jokes, and Fun
Stories From Racing's Greats!

by Ronda Jackson Martin

© 1994 by Premium Press America

ISBN 0-9637733-5-6

Library of Congress Catalog Card Number 94-68978

Premium Press America books are available at special discounts for
bulk purchases for sales promotions, premiums, fundraising, or
educational use. For information contact Premium Press America,
P.O. Box 159015, Nashville, TN, or call 800/891-7323.

Cover design by L. Mayhew Gore Art

Design by Lori E. Strickland, SET TO GO

Printed by Douglas Printing, Nashville, Tennessee

Reprinted January 1996
2 3 4 5 6 7 8 9 10

To All The Saturday Night Racers
Who Never Became Legends But Made
It Possible For Those Who Have

ACKNOWLEDGEMENTS

There are so many people I must thank for their assistance, whether they know they contributed or not. Thanks to Humpy Wheeler for telling me this was a great idea; Buck Baker for giving me the first interview and recommending me to his other racing friends; Cale Yarborough for the artistic license; Tom Higgins for being my hero; Waddell for his kindness; Henry Benfield for giving me the biggest laugh with that rubber snake on Atlanta's pit road; Doyle Ford for every story he told me on the record (and off the record!). And every legend that took the time to be a part of this book.

INTRODUCTION

When Wendell Scott died, I remember thinking of all the wonderful racing history and stories he took to the grave with him. It was then that I realized that a book needed to be written to record the memories of the racing family and save them for decades to come.

Conducting the interviews and writing this book has been the most rewarding experience I've ever had. I have met some of the most intelligent, kind, and personable people anyone could have the pleasure to have known.

Listening to these stories has been so much fun! I still giggle when I think about Kip McCord chasing Tommy Ellis around the infield with a Baby Ruth candy bar on the end of a stick, telling him it was dog 'droppings'! And I marvel at the ingenuity and brilliance of teams putting dry ice in the engine to chill the gas, or disconnecting the radiator fan in time trials to get more RPM's.

These men took their valuable time to contribute to this book, often at the track while preparing for qualifying or before a race that was to begin in an hour. One even took time during the week before Daytona to sit down and share his memories. Not only I, but all racing fans who read this book, are indebted.

Special thanks to the Charlotte Motor Speedway for introducing me to live racing by employing me in the suites; to Tracy May, Jay Sellars and Ibby for sharing my racing excitement; Greg, Tina and kids and Michelle Blaylock; Chip Litaker; Debbie Bodie, Deborah Moose, Lori Rusher, Karen Mallory, Char and Jennifer Ray for the friendship; FilMar Racing for assistance; Fil Martocci; Tom Hennigan; Bob Hice; Stan Blaylock, professional pilot/proofreader; Michael Benson and Toby Horton; Bob Weeks and Chip Williams; Kim and Kenny Wallace—you're the best; George Schnitzer; Bari Gant for computer support; and to my family, Mom, Lee, and my father-in-law PC, for the patience and support. God has blessed me greatly.

Especially to the best thing to ever happen to me—my best friend and husband Gil Martin. Without him this book would never have become a dream, a plan, an effort and finally a reality. You're my hero.

Mostly, thanks to the Good Lord from whom all blessings flow.

P.S. I love you Ford!

Contents

BUCK BAKER

Driver/Car Owner/Driving School Owner

The Baker name is deeply rooted in NASCAR racing. The patri-arch of the 'Fabulous Baker Boys' is Buck Baker, a legend in stock car racing. Buck, father of Winston Cup Champion Buddy Baker and driver Randy Baker, was NASCAR's Grand National (now Winston Cup) Champion for the years 1956 & '57, and first runner up to that title in '55 and '58. Retired after winning 46 races, he now operates the Buck Baker Driving School, located outside of Charlotte, North Carolina.

Buck Baker . . .

"I remember one particular time in Darlington, there was this sprint car driver—name was Henneshize, I believe. He was a good ol' fella, had a good sense of humor, too.

"See, when we raced back then we didn't have seat belts or roll bars in the car, so when you wrecked, you hung on for dear life!

"Well, ol' Henneshize got caught up in an accident, and through all the scraping and banging and smoke, I couldn't believe my eyes! This leg comes flying out of his window! Women began fainting and falling all about, and Henneshize was yelling, 'My leg! My leg! Somebody get my leg!'

"This one gentleman ran over to get it, kind of reluctantly, 'cause who wants to pick up a part of someone else's body that's fallen off? The old guy picked it up and looked at it, and had this kinda confused look on his face. Seems the leg had a 'Wynn' decal sticker on it! Heck . . . Henneshize had an artificial leg! But he sure did watch out for the 'Wynn' sponsor, didn't he?!

"I remember Junior Johnson was one of the best shine runners ever was, and a good shine runner's first instinct is when your car wrecks, then you get out and take off running because more than likely the law was following you.

"So, Junior was running real well in Daytona one year during a race, and flipped his car. I thought I would split my sides laughing at Junior crawling out of his car, lookin' white as a sheet and running for the hills!

"We used to have a bunch of fun in the different towns we traveled to. One time, in South Boston, Virginia, we couldn't find a hotel room cause the town was so small, so we went over to Danville to stay the night. The race had gotten rained out and so we just sat around the room and drank . . . nothing else to do.

"This friend of mine, Neil Castle and I, thought we'd go take a walk in the rain, and leave our other drinking buddy asleep, or passed out, in the room while we went out looking for trouble. But there wasn't anything around town except this ol' horse that was in a pasture across from the hotel.

"The horse was pretty gentle, and seemed to like us two drunk racers, so we took it on back to the hotel. We managed to get this horse up in our room, and real gentle-like woke up our sleeping partner laying in the bed.

"He wakes up in a stupor, and sees this big ol' horse standing right over his bed! This fella gets up and takes off so fast it would make your head spin! He jumped out of the bed in one move and ran straight into the wall, hollerin' and cussin' us the whole time!

"We had fun at the track, too. Bill France, Sr. called me one time

BUCK BAKER

and asked if I was coming to Daytona for the next race. I said, yeah—why do you wanna know? He said he figured he'd go ahead and post my bail now to beat the traffic!

"One guy that was always good for a laugh was Curtis Turner. He and Joe Weatherly were always into something. One time, while Joe was strapped into his car, Curtis ran up to him and threw in a giant pack of lit firecrackers right in his lap! You should have seen Joe trying to get out of that car with all of those fireworks going off, and Curtis doubled over laughing!

"Boy, I used to think I was real hot stuff out there on the racetrack. There was this one particular time, I had this white uniform I raced in that I dearly loved, and I wore it with pride every race. Maybe I was a little too proud, cause the radio announcers would never talk about me . . . that kind of made me mad.

"Anyway, I really had a liking for tomato juice, and I fixed myself up a thermos of it to ride in the car with me and sip on. Well, I was racin' right along, and then all at once, this car comes at me from nowhere and I 'T-boned' him broadside. Then, that thermos busts open and my tomato juice goes everywhere.

"It got off with me right bad because I broke my thermos, but the worst part was that my white uniform was ruined with tomato juice all over it! I climbed out of the car, and then the ladies in the stands all started swooning, and not because of my good looks!

"The radio was talking about me a hundred miles an hour, and I was getting all the attention. I looked up and waved at the stands, and they all applauded ... seems the guys on the radio were speculating and saying I was hurt real bad, and that my uniform was drenched in blood! So I guess I finally got those fellas on the radio to cover me!

"I've got a beautiful young wife now, I met her when she was a race queen. I'd do anything in the world for her, but there has been a time when I wasn't the best husband that ever was. Sometimes I'd get hooked up after a race with some of my wild buddies, and maybe a stray woman or two would show up, wanting to party with a race driver.

"One time when I was married to my second wife, instead of

going home after a race one night, I decided to go to a party and enjoy some drinks, music and maybe some ladies. The only problem was that some of the ladies didn't have a ride to get to the party, and we needed a car to pick them up.

"Well, Chevy had just sent me a new car that was sitting in my driveway, but I couldn't get it without waking her up. She was a tough woman, handy with a gun, and everybody was afraid of her—the last thing I wanted her to know was I was headed to a party and not home where I should have been.

"So one of my buddies says, 'Why don't you just bump your car out of gear and roll it out of the driveway so your wife will never know it's gone?' So we did. Ha—she saw every move we made!

"She gets in her car and real discreetly follows us to the garage, where the party was. She watches us go in with the women, and then parks the car on the street and walks up to the garage. Well, wouldn't you know the front of the building has glass windows all around the front, and she peeks in and sees everything we were up to.

"So she butts a hole in the glass with her pistol and begins to shoot at every woman she sees! People are running and hollering and diving under anything they can to dodge the bullets, and I see my wife and yell 'What the heck are you doing?!'

"She hollers back, without missing a shot, 'It's open season on prostitutes!' Then this cute little darlin' who broke one of her high heels, clip-clopped up to me and all scared to death with these big eyes and asks, 'What do I do??'

"I look at her as I'm running for cover and scream, 'Honey, run like there's no tomorrow!'

"Even my own kids were afraid of her, my second wife. Everybody in North Carolina knew about her reputation of being talented with a gun. She carried it with her everywhere she went. She also knew me pretty well, and she was always trying to catch me foolin' around on her.

"I remember one time, my son Buddy and I were driving back from a race, and I look in the rear view mirror. There she was! She pulled up beside us and shook her finger at me. Buddy immediately dives to the floor of the car and yells, 'Oh My Lord! She's got that gun again!'

7

"One of the greatest things about being in racing is watching your sons follow you in their career choice. I was a pretty proud man when Buddy won that Winston Cup race, but I feel just as proud of all my children.

"But just because you win a race, doesn't mean you can't make mistakes, though. There was one race in Talladega, Alabama, where Buddy was in the lead, driving an old winged Dodge, and a shoe-in to win the race with only a few laps remaining.

"All at once the yellow flag came out, making the race finish under caution. Buddy's pit held up a sign. That Buddy, I had always told him not to worry about the pits, to keep his eyes on the track in front of him.

"So he comes around, and looks in the pits and is so busy trying to read that sign, he runs right into the pace car! I mean loses the race! That got off with him so bad, he just had to run over to that pit board to see what it said.

"There it was in big letters ... 'We've got it made now! We've won!'"

HENRY BENFIELD

Truck Driver, Junior Johnson Racing

Henry has been transporting the #11 cars of Junior Johnson for over 10 years. He began working with Johnson's team in early 1970, and as Henry puts it, Junior and Flossie Johnson "practically raised me." When Henry isn't driving the rig for the Johnson team, he drives his own sportsman race car. Known as one of the best practical jokers in the Winston Cup garage area, there's not a soul in NASCAR that would say a bad word against this well-liked personality . . . although some have said they owe him a "payback or two."

Henry Benfield . . .

"Well, I've been in this garage a long time. Had quite a few drivers I've worked with. Some can take a joke a little better than others. But I guess you could pretty much say that about anybody. Don't matter where I am—if the mood strikes me, I'll pull a stunt. Some are planned out, some ain't.

"Like that restaurant we went to in Atlanta in '93 before the big blizzard hit and cancelled the race. I was with Elliott's team and I had a few stink bombs with me. There were several large 'fleshy' women around and I kinda casually dropped the bomb on the floor, stood aside and waited for the fun to begin.

"All at once, you could see the looks on these women's faces change. Their eyes started getting big and their noses wrinkled up and then all hell broke loose. They were coughing and putting their hands over their faces and yelling, 'Lawdy Mercy! Somebody done blowed double gas in here! Lawd, he'p us all . . . Weeze gotta get outta here! Who done blowed that double gas?!?!'

"They all scrambled for their coats, and hauled their fat butts out of that restaurant without paying their tab, causing a commotion all through the place. And they weren't the only ones that left—that bomb pretty much cleaned that joint out!

"As for the drivers, I've picked on all of 'em. I've put grease on Sterling Marlin's steering wheel right before practice. I've messed with Terry Labonte's carburetor and put oil on it to make it smoke.

"I remember when I was driving a long trip to a California race,

10

somebody gave me some 'stay awake' pills. Speed, I guess you could call them. So I figured, I ain't messed with Geoff Bodine in a while, so I dropped a couple in his water jug the next week in Pocono. Geoff never knew it at the time. Well, doncha know, that fella laid it to the floor and went on to win the race! He wanted to wring my neck when he found out!

"I guess I do have a reputation as a practical joker. Folks seem to expect it from me, I reckon. In 1978, I was working with Cale Yarborough. I didn't know I was pulling a stunt on him, but it worked out pretty well!

"We were at Charlotte Motor Speedway in May. It was the 600 lapper, and a driver can get good and thirsty on a hot Sunday afternoon in North Carolina. I had cleaned out Cale's water jug and had washed it real good, with liquid dish detergent. But I forgot to rinse it. So later I went on to fill it up with ice water, and put it in his car.

"Everything was going well, and then after 20-25 laps Cale came through on the radio and said 'Confound you, Henry Benfield!'

11

Of course he first hollered for me—'What have you done to my water! I'm out here blowing doggone bubbles!'

"I like most all of the drivers. I'm particularly fond of Kenny Schraeder. I'd venture to say that this man has helped me more than anyone else on this circuit. And not only can he take a good joke, he can come back with one!

"We were in Darlington and I believe it was in 1989. We were out by the pool at the hotel and had a cooler of beer on ice, playing cards and generally flappin' our jaws.

"Schraeder was out there talking to us and all at once I decided to throw him in the pool, clothes and all. He took it well and laughed it off. Well, a little later, Schraeder snuck up on me and without me knowing it, dumped the whole cooler of ice water on me! Everybody 'bout fell out laughing, and that water was so cold I thought I'd pass out! It took my breath away!

"Another favorite of mine was Tim Richmond. He may have been a bit 'Hollywood,' but he sure had a big ol' heart. A real good person inside all that polish. I remember one time Tim found a

12

homeless man that looked like he hadn't had a bath or a meal in weeks. Well, that 'bout broke Tim's heart in two and he decided he was going to buy this man the biggest steak dinner he'd ever had.

"So Tim brings him in this restaurant and sits him down, and the guys about have to bite a hole in their lips to keep from laughing . . . the poor old homeless man hasn't got any teeth! But Tim recouped real well and offers the old fella anything he wants to eat. Boy . . . I sure do miss Tim.

"I like all the crew members in the garage area. I know y'all have heard it a million times, but it really is like having a big family. We fight among ourselves, but let a stranger mess with one of us and he'll have to deal with all of us.

"Some of my favorite pals to get on a joke would be the crew of the #15 car (Bud Moore Racing). Especially Harold, Phil and Charlie. They know me well and have learned to be kind of wary when I'm around. Why, I'll bet you if I was to go up to their house and knock on the door, they might not even let me in . . . and we're old friends!

"We were in Darlington a few years ago, and I went up to their hotel room door and knocked. They were inside playing cards, and saw it was me, but wouldn't let me in. So I figured a good way to get around that.

"I got a real cute girl to go up and knock on the door while I hid behind her. That got 'em to open up and when they did I jumped out and threw a real long pack of lit firecrackers in their room, then I slammed the door and held it shut.

"You should have heard the hootin' and the hollerin' that was going on in that room above the loud popping and cracking of the firecrackers! Soon as I heard the last pop, I took off and the boys poured out of the room with a big ol' cloud of smoke behind them, coughing and carrying on and yelling for me!

"But the teams ain't the only ones that I play around with. I get to the NASCAR officials, too. I got Official Walter Wallace good in Talladega one time. I found a giant pair of women's underwear in a truck stop—I believe they were a size 80—and asked for some help from a hotel maid. She let me in Wallace's room, and I stashed the panties in his dirty laundry.

"Well, the next week he kept goin' on about these huge panties his wife found in his suitcase, and how she raised $300 worth of heck at him! I did finally get around to letting him in that it was me that tricked him. Somehow, he didn't seem too surprised!

"I pulled that same trick on a another friend of mine. In 1978, we were in College Station, Texas, and I bought a pair of ladies' pantyhose to put in his dirty clothes bag.

"Now, his wife had been accusing him of cheating on her for awhile. So one day when he was at work, he got a phone call at the office from his wife. She was screaming into the phone, 'I don't mind washing your clothes, but I'll be darned if I'm gonna wash HERS!' I believe that stunt cost him a divorce and a half a million dollars . . .

"We had one official, John, who is a great guy but was a bit naive. He was always nervous that his wife would think he was out doing something he wasn't supposed to be doing. So when he told me that, I headed myself down to the nearest drugstore to pick up a big 'ol box of condoms.

"The next time I was in John's car, I stuffed a bunch of them over the visor of the passenger seat when he wasn't looking. Imagine the heck he caught when he and his wife were driving around one afternoon and she pulled down the visor to look in the mirror, and all those rubbers fell in her lap!

"In Rockingham back in '88, I was able to get all of the officials at one time. I just fixed up a big pan of brownies, but rather than using real chocolate, I just substituted that chocolate laxative instead . . . I believe it was about 20 packs.

"I took 'em to the NASCAR truck, and those boys cleaned out that pan but fast! I do believe that put them out of commission for about a week or so!

"That idea came from the time we were at a Grand National party in '73. I was handing out that ladies' laxative that comes in the form of chewing gum to anyone who would take it, passing it off as real gum. One sweet little race queen got a bit greedy and took more than she needed to make a mouthful, and the poor thing wasn't able to make the race the next day!

HENRY BENFIELD

"My advice to those that have read about this is: Don't try these pranks at home . . . they can cause more trouble than it's worth. Or—learn to run awful fast!"

BILL BRODRICK

Unocal Public Relations

Bill Brodrick has been involved with motorsports for over 26 years, beginning with a job at a Newport, Kentucky, radio station covering NASCAR. He began handling the public relations for Unocal's racing division in January of 1969, to represent the company in all motorsports events. His position as 'victory lane director' evolved from track operators requesting his organizational skills. "Every victory lane event is different . . . I love it."

Bill Brodrick . . .

"I remember back in Rockingham, North Carolina, David Pearson was driving for the Wood Brothers racing team. It was a 500 mile race, but that day it was extremely cold. And when the weather is cold like that, the drivers tend not to perspire as they do on hot days, thus retaining more water.

"Well, as soon as David got out of the car in victory lane, he muttered to me, 'Hurry and get this over with . . . I've gotta go!'

19

Well, he shouldn't have told me that. With sheer delight I did everything I could do to keep him as long as I could, with photos and interviews! Finally, David threw up his hands and said, 'That's it!' and ran off towards the restrooms!

"One driver I really thought a lot of was Tim Richmond. He knew the value of the media, had the savvy, and enjoyed the publicity. I'd always point out the wire service to him in victory lane and he'd follow my direction. Yep, he enjoyed the press and played it to the hilt. He liked to spray the champagne and knew how to take a picture . . . in fact, he 'made' photos happen.

"Another driver that I got a kick out of was Buddy Baker. See, Buddy loved to win, but for some reason, victory lane made him sick. I mean, physically ill . . . nauseated! This man could drive a car over 200 mph, but victory lane freaked him out.
"One time in particular, he drove into victory lane and told me, 'I'm gonna barf!' So I tried to calm him down, but he kept telling me he was going to throw up. Finally, he did throw up—all over

himself and his car! We had to clean him up before he got out of the car and made photos.

"David Pearson was so much fun. One time I was in South Carolina, and I rode to the track with him. We were racing in Darlington that weekend, and we were driving clear across the state from Spartanburg, David's home town.

"Well, there was a restaurant across from the track, the Speedway Grill, and it was our favorite place to eat lunch. We were really pushing it to get there by noon. So, knowing how frugal Pearson is, I told him, 'You're not gonna make it by noon.' He assured me we would, so I said, 'O.K.—if we're there before noon, I'll buy lunch, but if it's after noon, you buy!'

"We were on Route 50, where it turns into four lanes for about 20 miles, and David figures he's got a free lunch coming. But all at once David slows down. Seems there was a highway patrolman up ahead, and David had to fall in behind him. I never before have heard such moaning for 20 miles . . . yep, he had to follow that cop for the full 20 miles!

"The best part is that we were just a little past noon arriving at the Speedway Grill, and I got the free lunch!

"If I could offer anyone any advice I wish I'd been given, it is to never get into a race car with a race driver. In 1969, I was once again in Darlington, and at the end of the day of practice, LeeRoy Yarbrough asked me if I wanted to go around the track with him for a couple of laps.

"So I said, yeah, why not? Well, I was on the right side, where there is no seat, and not much room for a passenger, so I wrapped myself around the roll bars. We went out and ran a couple of neat laps. But when it was time to go in, Lee Roy decided to floor it, and 'parked' the car on the wall between turn three and four.

"There I was with no helmet on, and scared half to death! He thought it was so funny! I've not done that since!

"Davey Allison was a special person. He had a large family, and whenever he won, victory lane was always crowded with cousins, aunts, uncles and other relatives. He also had all of his friends there to help celebrate. The winner's circle would always be packed with young folks. Just like his father had when he won, but younger people.

"Davey would always make sure he took pictures with everybody, and he would always be in the best mood. He looked after everybody else, and never, ever took the glory for himself.

"Alan Kulwicki was a great racer, too. But whenever he was in victory lane, he never got out of his car without looking in his rear view mirror, taking out a comb, and combing his hair. Even if we were running late on time for the television broadcasts, Alan didn't care. He wasn't getting out of that car until every hair was in place!

"I also enjoy the 'race stoppers,' the name we gave our Unocal girls we have as representatives in victory lane. We first introduced them in 1969 at the Daytona 500. We even had nine at one time, but after the energy crunch of '74 we had to cut back.

"I kind of shepherd all of the girls. You have no idea what it's like being in the car with three or four girls putting on makeup at the same time. I've zipped zippers, fastened fasteners, and car ried more hairdryers than I can remember. It's like having several wives but none of the benefits!

"But we don't do bikinis. Never have, never will. We go for the family approach. That's what makes us so successful as a family sport, wouldn't you agree?"

CEO and Chairman of the Board
Martinsville Speedway, Virginia

Clay Earles has a rich history behind him in racing. Born and reared in Martinsville, he single-handedly began what is now home to the Hanes 500 and Goody's 500 Winston Cup races. One of the original NASCAR tracks, it opened in 1947 as a dirt track and was paved in 1955. Located on Highway 220 South, two miles outside of Martinsville, Virginia, towards the North Carolina border, it is a .526 mile track—the smallest track in its venue. Clay, one of the most powerful and influential men in NASCAR, believes his success comes from one commitment: honesty.

Clay Earls . . .

"I built this track back in 1947, even before NASCAR was born. They came about two years later, but I built it before I knew about the idea of NASCAR. I had seen a small dirt track outside of North Carolina that seated about three thousand people.

"I was turned on by it and the idea of building one myself, thinking this is what I might need to get into as a hobby and a money maker. So I looked around for suitable land and decided on this place here.

"Heck, back then there was no access except for a dirt road, but it was a nice piece of 35-acre land. A good friend of mine had a dirt moving company and I talked him into going in with me, and he brought along another friend as a partner. The men were Sam Rice and Henry Lawrence.

"We didn't put much money into it at first, maybe twenty thousand each, but by the time we held our second race, we had over one hundred thousand dollars in it together—which was a lot of money in 1947!

"Sam and Henry stayed with me until 1952. By then they were bored with it and had no interest, and I had to do it all myself. So I bought them out. Bill France approached me soon after that, and talked to me about forming a sanctioning body.

"I had met Bill in Daytona, where he had a gas station on Main Street. Well, I had already held one sanctioned race at my track, in the Triple A division. They were nice folks, they advertised me—but that was the only Triple A race I promoted because it was a total failure! The public had no interest in it. In fact, a great driver named Ted Horn ran in that race, and he was killed later that fall.

"Well, Bill came up around 1950 or '51, cause he wanted to see my track. He says to me, 'Clay, how about me helping you?' He made an offer. He knew all of the drivers would run there, and we talked money and agreed to work together. So I ask him 'What else can you do?' and he tells me, 'I can park cars.' So I hired him to park cars. Can you believe that? The NASCAR President and founder parking cars!

"Later there were beach races, and Bill put on a few, but he lost money on concessions. I knew about concessions, so I offered to help him set that up. We made quite a few thousand on that. Then I built those carnival-type tear-down stands to put on the beach and did that for about three years. It was quite successful for us. But I had to give that beach business up later, so Bill hired a concession company to run it. And I went home to Virginia.

"In 1955, I called Bill and told him I planned to pave the track. Do you know what he told me? He said, 'Clay, don't you think you'll ruin it?' Ha! Can you believe that? I told him I wasn't making any money with dirt, and I had to. So I paved it and in the fall of '55, I had in attendance twice as many people than I'd had for any prior race.

"Since then, we've done exceptionally well. The seats I added recently cost over a million dollars. I was fortunate enough to be able to buy up all of the available land adjacent to the track, and now that totals over 200 acres.

"In the late '50s and early '60's, I was a representative for NASCAR. There was no Virginia sanctioned NASCAR track at the time. Pat Purcell was the manager of NASCAR then, and he was the type of man who would tell you what you must do, not make a suggestion or request.

"He called a meeting in Richmond for all of the promoters, and made a speech, saying he wanted them to join NASCAR. He ended the speech by saying, 'I am advising you to come with us. If you don't, we'll put you out of business. Now, do you want to come?'

"Not one track went with him! So I held a meeting two or three weeks afterward, and talked to all of the promoters. I signed every track except one, and I had that one in six weeks!

"But things have not always gone smoothly for NASCAR. Back in the early '60's, Curtis Turner was a Grand National Driver, now Winston Cup, and he was in with the Teamsters Union. He wanted to form a union with the drivers. We would have never stayed in business if that happened.

"Millions of dollars in tickets could be sold ahead of time, and to reimburse because of a strike would have been difficult to say the least. Bill, Sr. came to me and asked me, 'What can you do?' I told him I'd tell the promoters what we were up against. He OK'd that plan, so I held meetings, telling everyone who would listen that there was no place for a union in NASCAR. The fans are honest with us and we must guarantee them a race.

"I also talked to the drivers. I told them, 'If you have a problem, forget the union—just come and tell me—I'll get it done! But if you stay in the union, I'll put a lock on my gate and all of the promoters will put a lock on their gate and where will you be?' They all dropped out within a month.

"Curtis didn't like that one bit and tried to push us, so I suspended him from NASCAR for 'conduct unbecoming a NASCAR member.' Well, he was out for awhile, but we allowed him back in later. And he never mentioned 'union' again.

"I am thankful for my success, but I don't believe I've lucked into it. I have always been honest with folks, done what I have promised, and paid my debts. I have never had any problems following those rules, and to this day I can go to any bank in this area and know I can get a loan for any amount on my word.

"Like the commercial says, 'You keep giving the people what they want and do it fairly, and they'll keep coming back.' It isn't me that has made Martinsville a success—it's the fans of racing."

DOYLE FORD

Official NASCAR Starter/Flagman

Doyle Ford is a character. With a quick smile and a quicker wit, Doyle has been a part of NASCAR racing for years. He learned his duties from the late great Harold Kinder, a flagstand fixture for decades. Doyle began as the assistant starter, and took over the position when Kinder retired. Ford also owns a security system company and resides in Nashville, Tennessee.

Doyle Ford . . .

"Sometimes I think maybe my job is a little more dangerous than people think. I've never been hit by anything—at least nothing serious—but sometimes I'll hear things whizz by my ears, and it has that whoosh sound, kind of like a boomerang.

"I have come off of the stand bleeding like a stuck pig, but just from little ol' stinging stuff that don't hurt. But my number board has been smashed to smithereens by what I assume was wheel weights or lug nuts . . . at least that's what it looked like. That's close.

31

"I've never to my knowledge had a driver mad at me for a black flag. Some of them have waved at me with one finger, or shaken their fist at me, or come up to me after the race and said, 'Why didn't you get car so-and-so . . . he was two laps down and he was in the way!'

"I have a standard answer for that question: 'Why don't you get me a remote control for that car and I'll steer it!' See, at first the flags were just informational flags, it wasn't a must-do. But now it's a rule.

"Also, I don't have the latitude to black flag a car for a procedural violation. That's up to the race director that sits behind me directly upstairs. I can black flag them for danger, like losing fluids or sheet metal dangling. But I take my directions from the race director upstairs. And that gets me off the hook for some of the blame, too!

"I first got my first official's license with NASCAR in 1959 at the old fairgrounds speedway in Nashville. I raced two years on dirt, but I never was a 'race car driver.' I probably never drove over 12 races in my entire life.

"I started out in Nashville on the clean-up crew, and when we were NASCAR sanctioned, I was made an inspector. Soon the assistant starter left, and I was asked to replace him. I eventually moved up to starter in the mid-1960's. I began backing Harold Kinder in '78, and took over when Harold left in May 1990.

"My first official duty as Winston Cup chief starter was not to flag a Winston Cup race, but to flag the Winston Open, and then The Winston. Now, these are not officially Winston Cup races. So my first official Cup race was the '600.'

"There was a reporter that caught me in Charlotte for an interview, and through his questions about my background, was perhaps trying to establish in his own mind what my qualifications were to be the Winston Cup Chief Starter.

"He said, 'I get the distinct feeling that you're not really enthused with your new appointment as starter.' I told him I didn't know where he got that from, that of course I was enthused and honored with the position.

"I had to explain to him that the prestige I received was being able to represent NASCAR, and not what I do within the team that makes me proud. We don't have any unimportant or unnecessary jobs in NASCAR—NASCAR is a team, and I'm proud to be a part of that team.

"Most of the funny stuff I can tell in public happened with Harold Kinder, cause Harold was a hoot. You know the expression 'The B.S. stops when the green flag drops'? Well, that ain't necessarily so!

"Harold and I had a lot of fun during the race. But we never, ever lost sight of our reason for being there on the flagstand. We didn't always have spotters, which is one of the best things NASCAR ever implemented. So we took our job seriously.

"One of the funniest things I can remember was when Telly Savalas, from the TV show 'Kojak,' was the honorary starter at Charlotte one year. Harold and I were joking around with him on the flagstand, because being up there can be kind of intimidating for some one who has never been up there before.

"Telly was a bit apprehensive from the start. This was before they built the new flagstand. This flagstand just protruded through the fence, and there was a cable that went right above our head.

"Well, Harold gave them the one-to-go, and I was standing behind Telly. Harold looked around to me, laughing, and pointed up to the cable, where Savalas was holding on to it . . . and the

DOYLE FORD

poor man's knuckles had turned white! He was holding on to that cable like he knew he was surely gonna fly off of the flagstand!

"Telly saw us laughing and said, 'What are you guys laughing at?' Harold giggled and said, 'Are you scared?' and Telly said, 'Of course I'm scared!' And Harold said, 'Well, Kojak, I watch you on television and you ain't afraid of nothing!' Telly told him, 'Well, buddy, that television is play-like, and this stuff here is REAL!'

"Another time at Charlotte we had country performer Charlie Daniels as honorary starter. We got up on the flagstand and Charlie had this big ol' chew of tobacco in his mouth. Harold told Charlie what he was going to do and how and when. I said, 'Charlie, you got all that stuff down?' and Charlie said 'Yep.' I said, 'Well, there's one thing that Harold didn't tell you. If you drop that green flag on that racetrack, you're gonna have to go get it!'

"Well, he looked at me and wallered that old tobacco around and finally said, 'Hmm . . . appears to me, since you're the ones that's got a need for that flag, if you want it, **YOU** go get it! I ain't goin' down there!' He was dead serious, too . . . he knew that flag was more important to me than it was him!

35

"Harold was a great man, and Harold was innovative. In fact, the flagstand at Charlotte was dedicated to him and is known as the 'Kinder Stand.' It has a bronze plaque on it in memory of Harold. In fact, when the people in Charlotte took over Atlanta, the very next race they had transformed their flagstand into the same type of stand. But there is only one Kinder Stand, at Charlotte.

"Harold got to see the Kinder Stand built, and got to flag from it, and boy, that made his chest puff out . . . he was really proud of that, as well he should be.

"He used to play with some of the drivers, the race leaders in particular. If someone was leading the race by a comfortable margin, Harold would play with them.

"You know, I think it would surprise most people to know how good we actually can see the drivers' faces from the flagstands, even for the short times they are in view. Most now wear the full face shields, so you can't see as well anymore, but back then they mostly wore goggles and you could pretty much read their expressions.

"Well, one time Darrell Waltrip was leading a race by a good margin. Harold turned to me and said, 'Hey—watch ol' Darrell.' Harold leaned over when D.W.'s car approached and waved at him with his right hand. Darrell waved at him with his right hand.

"Next lap, Harold told me to watch and then waved at him with his left hand. Darrell did the same, waving at him with his left hand. But the next lap around, Harold waved at Darrell with both hands. Darrell just looked at Harold and when he came around again, he waved at us with one finger! But it of course is all done in fun.

"Now Buck Baker's son is a memory from Talladega. I was backing Harold, and for some reason we black-flagged Buddy Baker. Well, he wouldn't come in, so we finally got him on pit road. He thought he had been handed punishment far exceeding what he thought he deserved and he was upset.

"He comes down pit road waving at us with one finger, big time! Then the race director called down to us and said, 'Harold Kinder, did Buddy Baker do what I think he just did?' Harold, who didn't want to get anyone into trouble, says, 'Well, I think he was just

37

waving at us.' The director said, 'Naw, he did exactly what I thought he did!'

"So he called the official on pit road and said to have Buddy see him in his office immediately when the race was over. Well, they fined Buddy one thousand dollars for making obscene gestures.

"We then moved on to Charlotte, and Buddy was there. He comes out of his truck to go to his car with his drivers uniform on, and instead of having his fireproof driver's gloves on, he was wearing a pair of mittens.

"Some one said, 'Say, Buddy . . . are you gonna drive in those mittens?' Buddy said, 'Well, yea, my car owner is making me . . . he figured with these, I wouldn't cost him another thousand dollars!'

"Another funny Buddy Baker-Talladega story concerns the layover flag. Buddy has always despised the layover flag. Now, of course, most of the time Buddy was never given the layover flag. He was usually the one the layover flag was given for, because

Buddy always ran very well. But regardless, he hated that flag.

"Well, one time at Talladega, he was real low on the grass, and he was just warming up his car. There was not another car in sight of him in either direction, and he was only going about 70-80 miles per hour, which looks like you're crawling at Talladega.

"I saw him coming out of that tri-oval and he was hugging the grass down there warming up, so I showed him that layover flag and I worked that thing just as hard as I could work it! He kept up his same speed on the grass all around the racetrack, came on into pit road, and really lowerated that official on pit road . . .

"He said, 'You tell that dumb, stupid flagman that I was going slow because I was warming my car up and I was already down on the grass! If I had 'layovered' any further I'd have been in the infield—and besides that, there wasn't another car in sight! So why was he giving me the layover flag?' Had I not known how much he hated that flag I wouldn't have thought of doing it. I got the biggest kick out of that one!

"I was flagging practice one time and Marty Robbins was driving. He was on the race track and we were at Talladega, and the drivers, before they qualify, like to practice alone, cause that's how they qualify . . . alone. And they want to get a feel for the track with no other cars around.

"So Marty was out there by himself, and there wasn't another car in sight. I got all eight of the flags in my hands and I fanned them out between all of my fingers, holding eight different colored flags. When Marty got close to the flagstands, I waved all of them . . . every one of them!

"He backed off his car when he went into turn one, I mean he backed off immediately when I put those flags out. He crept slowly down the back straightaway, thru three and four and came down pit road, where he eased down to the official who works pit road and stopped.

"After a few minutes the official keyed his microphone on his headset and said, 'Uh, Doyle . . . Marty wanted to know what flag was that you put on him? Says he ain't never seen a flag that color before!'

"We've had a lot of stuff happen at Pocono. We've had dogs, turtles, 'bout everything imaginable on the racetrack at Pocono. One particular time there, a safety crew member reported to the tower that there was a deer lingering dangerously close to the racing surface . . . he was not on the racetrack, but was close enough to cause concern. The tower told him to watch it closely and if it got any closer, speak up.

"Well, Harold looked at me and shrugged his shoulders. When the cars started coming around, Harold put the layover flag under his arm and put his fingers in a 'V' formation on both sides of his head in hopes the drivers would pick up that he was trying to mimic a deer. I don't know if they realized what he was doing, but they got a big kick out of it.

"Then, the last race of the '92 season at Pocono, a cleanup truck radioed in and said, 'Tower . . . this is Cleanup One located at the exit of pit road . . . and it seems we have a chicken on the race track.'

"There was a little pause on the radio, then NASCAR came on the radio and said, 'Cleanup One, would you repeat that?' 'Yes, Tower, we have a chicken on the race track, headed toward turn one!'

41

"I turned around and looked at the tower, which I could see very easily at Pocono, and they were just cracking up! I looked down at the track, and sure enough, there was something, but I could just barely see it. But I could see it was moving, and it was moving in the direction of turn one.

"I came on and said I could verify that there was something out there, just in case they thought it was a joke. So they told me to go ahead and put out a flag. I did, and got the cars slowed down behind the pace car.

"In a few minutes, Cleanup One came back on and says, 'Well, we got it, but it wasn't a chicken . . . it was a turkey!' And indeed it was a wild turkey—we had to stop a race to get a turkey off the race track . . . and this turkey wasn't driving a car, either!"

Motor Racing Network Sportscaster

Eli Gold has been a household name among racing fans for the last 20 years. "The Voice" of Motor Racing Network can be heard every Tuesday night on "NASCAR Live," his solely-hosted call-in radio talk show, every Winston Cup race broadcast on MRN, and on the syndicated television talk show "This Week In NAS-CAR." Want more of Eli? Then you'll be happy if you live in Alabama, where Eli calls play-by-play action for the University of Alabama football games. Eli Gold is the ultimate professional media authority for NASCAR racing.

Eli Gold . . .

"I believe I must say my favorite memory from the broadcast tower would be involving Ned Jarrett when he was our pit reporter several years ago. Ned covered the pits and garage area, and in the turns. He was very good at it, and knew all of the team members.

"Well, in one particular incident, Ned had told us he had to

43

relieve himself in the men's lavatory, and not to cut away to him in the pits if there was a pit stop. We acknowledged his absence and went about our business of continuing coverage of the race.

"Moments later, Richard Petty blew a tire and came into the pits. Ned's destination completely escaped me, and out of force of habit I said, 'Richard Petty is in for a tire change, let's go to Ned Jarrett in the pits.' I had completely forgotten where Ned was!

"Before I could cover myself, Ned, who had heard my faux pas on his headset, spoke up—covering the pit stop from the sanctity of the garage port-a-john! He knew from experience exactly what was going on in the pit for the tire change, and called the stop play-by-play, exactly the way it was happening! That to this day is one of the funniest things that has happened to me in this sport!

"Not to seem stuck on restroom memories, there was a time when all of the MRN racing audience was informed of my bodily functions!

"We have a radio crew that keeps MRN flowing smoothly, and one of the responsibilities they have is when we're coming back

44

from a commercial, they must inform us when the mike is hot. That means our microphone is on and in 10 seconds we're to resume coverage.

"At that time, I was a pit reporter working one of the turns, not as of yet working in my present position in the broadcast tower. I had to go to the restroom in a most serious way, and I mean I had to go badly.

"I told the crew up in the tower, in a most graphic and distasteful fashion, that I was headed to the restroom to relieve myself. Unfortunately, in my desperation, I had missed the information that the mike was hot, meaning I had informed all of the United States of America's MRN listening audience of my plight. No one had to wonder why Eli Gold was not heard from for the next few minutes!

"One thing this sport has afforded me is the opportunity to meet all types of people. Some of them were of dubious character, but some were a blessing. Davey Allison was a blessing.

"One weekend, I had just arrived at the North Wilkesboro airport straight from broadcasting an Alabama football game, and was headed to my hotel. It was about 6 p.m., the dinner hour, and I'm driving along minding my own business.

"All at once, this tremendous black truck comes upon me, almost running me off of the road. I'm honking, cursing and shaking my fists, and suddenly I realize it was Davey at the wheel, playing with me. Did I get angry? Heck, no. I laughed at him and we went to have dinner together!

"Finally, I feel I must relate this story to you. I'm not much of a practical joker . . . I leave that to the Henry Benfield. But I absolutely could not resist an opportunity I had recently in New Hampshire.

"New Hampshire is famous for their lobsters, and while there myself and a few friends decided to go try out the local seafood fare at a nearby restaurant. Well, I ended up eating a tremendous dinner of lobster, and all of the guys were giving me grief about it. The next day, I was still getting ribbed about it in the broadcast booth.

"So we're in the middle of the race, and Bobby Labonte was being interviewed by my associate, Winston Kelly, in the pits after a mishap of some sort. After talking out about his mechanical problems, Bobby added, 'By the way—there is an all points bulletin out for Eli Gold, who is said to be responsible for singlehandedly destroying the entire New Hampshire lobster population. If you see him, please turn him into the lobster authorities.'

"Well, I knew right away the only way he could have known about that deal was from Winston Kelly. So I laughed it off and continued with the coverage.

"But at the end of the broadcast where I thank the MRN crew, I grinned to myself and said, 'We would like to also thank Winston Kelly for his fine contribution to MRN, but this was Winston's final broadcast with us. Winston, you will be missed.'

"People called all week! The phones rang off of the hook wondering why Winston was leaving or if it was true!"

TOM HIGGINS

Motorsports Writer

Tom Higgins is one of the few motorsports writers in NASCAR that when you read his column, you can surely bet it's written on fact, not speculation and gossip. Perhaps that's why Tom has been covering NASCAR for The Charlotte Observer for the last 30 years. One of the most articulate and talented writers in stock car racing, it is no wonder he is the favorite among drivers and teams alike. Tom began his motorsports career 35 years ago, covering his first big race in 1958, the Southern 500. Hard work, tenacity, and a winning personality have established him as the most respected writer in the business, with a distinguished career full of awards.

Tom Higgins . . .

"I remember one time when David Pearson was qualifying his car at Bristol . . . I don't remember exactly which year, but it was in the '70's. Pearson was running for Holman-Moody back then, and he had gone out on the track, caught a cloud and qualified pretty high.

"Well, the only one that could possibly catch him was Bobby Isaac, and he was next to qualify. At that time, Bristol was fairly new, and there were still weeds and bushes in the infield.

"So when Isaac got on line to qualify, Pearson went and hid in the bushes off of the apron on turn three. Then, when Isaac got around the track, Pearson jumped out and was waving his arms at him. Isaac cracked the throttle—lifted off the gas—just enough for Pearson to beat him for the pole. Isaac came in and asked NASCAR 'What's wrong?'

"They said, 'What are you talking about?' Isaac said, 'Somebody waved me down over there in turn three!' They told him he was crazy, so he said, 'Well, then I get to run again.' NASCAR told him 'You're not running again, we don't know anything about anybody waving at you.'

"So Bobby got to asking around and found out it was Pearson. And although they were very, very good friends, Isaac exploded as only he could explode. He got a tire tool, as back then they weren't using air wrenches, and chased Pearson all over that infield . . . Pearson finally crawled under a truck to get rid of him! Heck, if he hadn't, Bobby might have killed him—or at least inflicted some serious damage!

"Pearson and Isaac were a real pair. Pearson had pulled so many practical jokes—Pearson was really clever, and Isaac was sort of, well, Isaac! But it got to where Pearson had pulled so many practical jokes on Isaac, that Isaac was looking for a way to get even.

"It was the Southern 500 weekend in Darlington, and Bobby had heard Pearson say he was going to have some sort of small party at his motel. Now, I don't know whether somebody put Isaac up to this or he thought it up on his own, but he called a local ice company, told them he was David Pearson, he was having a big party, and he wanted a truckload of ice delivered to the motel.

"This was back when they ran the race on Monday, and there were all kinds of antics that took place on Sunday because the track was closed.

"So Sunday afternoon this ice man shows up with a huge truckload of ice and went to Pearson. Well, Pearson had no idea what he was talking about. The race driver and the ice driver almost came to blows! And Isaac is in his room, cracking up watching the whole thing. The ice man finally drove off, but it was a major incident to behold.

"In another story about Bobby Isaac, he decided to take up the fine sport of golf. Richard Powers, who was then president of Charlotte Motor Speedway, started Bobby playing golf in the early '70's, and built a golf course up near where both of them lived— Westfork Country Club on Lake Norman, North Carolina.

"Isaac was left-handed, but he couldn't find any left-handed clubs, so he had to play right-handed. Well, the poor fellow couldn't hit a lick, and lost a lot of golf balls! So he started getting a caddy to go with him, and just playing by himself, trying to practice.

"On this course there was a very difficult water hole, and Isaac hit every ball he had in his golf bag in the water hole. There had to be twenty of his balls in the hole, one after the other, without ever getting one across.

"He became so frustrated, he took his bag off the golf cart and threw his bag of golf clubs into the water. But then he remembered he'd left his car keys in the golf bag!

"So here was Bobby, wading in to get the golf bag out! As he exited the water hole with his pants rolled up around his knees and his face as red as a beet, up on the green there was this kid, around high school age, that was just rolling on the grass laughing at him, watching the whole embarrassing scene.

"Bobby was still furious, so he went up to the kid, jerked him up by the seat of the pants and the back of the neck, and threw the kid in the lake too!

"One time, Cale Yarborough was rooming in the old Swamp Fox hotel in Florence with Tiny Lund. Back then, everyone saved expenses by rooming together. Tiny was in the shower, and Cale thought he'd be cute and pour ice cold water on Tiny.

"Now, the last time he did that, Tiny, buck-naked, chased Cale out of the hotel room. This time, Tiny was ready for it. Tiny jumped out of the shower, grabbed a laughing Cale, picked up him and the mattress—and threw them both into the hotel swimming pool! Once again, Tiny chose to do this in his birthday suit! I mean stark naked—didn't bother him a bit!

"Bill France, Sr. was a card, too. Steve Waid, another sportswriter, and I have laughed for years over all the pre-race prayers that we've heard, because it reminds us of the time Big Bill was to deliver the pre-race invocation at the Daytona 500.

"Big Bill called us all to prayer, and commenced the praying. He had a voice even deeper than mine—and he prayed and prayed and prayed. He prayed for everything you could imagine, and he beseeched the Lord for everything he could beseech him for.

"It was the longest prayer I believe I've heard before a race. Maybe a record, I don't know. He finally got to the end of it . . . and drew a mental blank! He couldn't remember one word, and that word was <u>Amen</u>! He could not remember the word Amen!

"There was this long silence. Finally, he said, so help me God, no pun intended—'Sincerely . . . Bill France'! That was the first time the press box ever laughed at a prayer.

"When ESPN did a tribute to Bill Sr., at his death, I was very flattered when they asked me to be a part of it and I told the same story. The Rev. Hal Marks came on after me, and he confirmed the incident—and told the rest of it as well!

"Rev. Marks said that afterward, Bill came over to them and his wife and said, 'Annie Bea, what's the word you're supposed to end prayers with?' And she tells him, 'It's 'Amen', Bill.' He turned his head in aggravation and said, 'That's it, G#*D@#! it! I couldn't think of what that word was!'

"I've got time for one more story. There was once a great old announcer named Gray Milton. He was corny, but he thought he was great. And this was back in the early days of Daytona, where they were using International Scout vehicles as service trucks that of course had been given to them, free of charge.

"Well, a most appreciative Bill, Sr. sent word to announcer Gray Milton to plug the International Scouts. But as the race wore on and wore on and wore on, Gray didn't say anything, so Bill, Sr. sent him another message to plug the International Scouts. Big Bill sent word to him about three or four times and Gray still didn't do it. Finally, he sent the message, 'Gray plug the International Scouts, or you're fired!'

"So moments later Gray broadcasts, 'Ladies and gentlemen, we're glad to have with us today a group of International Scouts. Stand up, boys, so we can give you a hand!'"

PHIL HOLMER

Goodyear Racing Field Manager

Whenever there is a question about stagger, tire construction, compound or tire pressure, Phil Holmer is the man that can provide the answer. Holmer is the field manager for Goodyear's Stock Car Racing Program. He began his racing career in 1967 as a sportswriter for The Orlando Sentinel, covering the Florida races. He was young and straight out of the army, and was given this beat to cover because "nobody else wanted to cover racing." Eighteen months later, because of his outstanding sportswriting, he was chosen to be the first Public Relations Manager for NASCAR. He stayed there until 1976, when he was brought aboard the Goodyear team. He is now respected in both the Busch Grand National and Winston Cup garage areas, and is often consulted by teams for assistance and opinions.

Phil Holmer . . .

"I believe one of my favorite memories is a particular night many years ago—I don't quite remember the year—when an occurrence took place that today would be completely unheard of.

"Back when I lived in Florida, I owned half interest in a nice little pub in Daytona Beach called the Boot Hill Saloon. Now it's a famous biker bar, but back then all we served was beer and wine. It was a neighborhood place, somewhere you wouldn't think twice about taking your kids to. It had a shuffleboard game there, and sometimes people would stay and play all night . . . we'd even have tournaments between the media and the racing guys.

"Well, my birthday was during Speedweek in February. My wife decided to surprise me that year with a birthday party in the bar. She told everyone—all of the drivers, media and press people, I mean everyone. And, of course, I had no idea . . . until I showed up that night. I was simply amazed at the people that were in attendance.

"There was Mark Donahue, who won the IROC race that afternoon and retired the same day; Buddy Baker and Benny Parsons playing shuffleboard; Johnny Rutherford; Bill James, of Car and Driver Magazine, and also Road and Track Magazine; southern sportswriters Joe Whitlock and Tom Higgins; Bill Brodrick, and so many others—just drinking beer, playing shuffleboard and having a great time. Something like that would never happen today. This was before the sport got so big. There are now so many demands on time, whether it be a media event, sponsor meeting, or autograph session.

"We all would get together often back then, to just socialize or play around. I remember we used to play beach volleyball together. Buddy Baker has always been in excellent shape, and he loved to play. Well, I got in a game with him one day and in the heat of the competitiveness, I went for a ball and landed with my heel right on Buddy's toe and broke it. He lost the race he was running that week and blamed it on me. You know, he still hasn't forgiven me for that!

"Now that Henry Benfield . . . he's always got something going. There's this fella with Champion Spark Plugs—his name is Earl, I believe. Henry used to always trick him by putting stink bombs in his car so when he'd crank up his car, the bomb would explode and this awful smell would emerge. The first few times this happened, Earl panicked and thought his car was blowing up. But he became used to the fact that his car was OK, but Henry wasn't! It almost got to the point where it was painful for Earl!

"There was always fun in the hotels, too. I remember one crew chief that had a history of all kinds of mischief—everything from being stuck in a Mexican jail to—well, let's just say he could find himself in all sorts of trouble if he looked hard enough. Not too many people know that he was a gymnast when he was younger.

"So one night when several of us met in the hotel lobby to go to dinner together, this particular guy came up to us after having a drink or two and told the guys in the group that he'd bet them money that he could walk out of that hotel lobby on his hands. He won the bet hands down—no pun intended! It got to where he'd make this bet in almost every hotel we stayed in. That was a sucker bet that everybody fell for!

"As for the drivers we had that left us before their time, I have nothing but fond memories. Like Tim Richmond. Wow, what a talent. I think he may be the only driver who intimidated Dale Earnhardt. He had such savvy, on and off the track. I would have loved to have seen where he'd gone in NASCAR. And Alan Kulwicki—he would sit and grill my engineers for hours on end for knowledge. I sure miss them both. But where one leaves off, another is soon to pick up. That's why we at Goodyear not only appreciate the Kulwickis and the Richmonds of the past, but also the Wallaces, Gordons, and Earnhardts of the future."

JIM HUNTER

President/General Manager — Darlington Raceway

Whoever said you can't come home again hasn't talked to 'Sand-lapper' Jim Hunter. Hunter is current President and GM of Darlington, the track 'too tough to tame.' He began his illustrious career in motorsports working in his beloved home state of South Carolina at the Columbia State newspaper as a sports journalist in the early '60's. He later moved to Darlington, where he headed up the public relations department of the 1.366 mile oval, which opened in 1950. After a stint at Talladega, he went on to NASCAR headquarters, where he remained for eleven years before returning home to the Palmetto state. Not only is he a well respected NASCAR authority, he is also the author of several racing-related books, such as 21 Forever: The David Pearson Story, Stock Car USA, and Racing to Win—Wood Brothers Style. He also has published several works on South Carolina football, including *Puppydogs, Pigtails and Pigskins.* Trivia fact: Jim Hunter, Charlotte's Humpy Wheeler, and NASCAR's Jim Duncan all three played football together on scholarships at the University of South Carolina.

Jim Hunter . . .

"I feel fortunate to be able to recall some truly wonderful memories to you. One of the best is a hysterical event that includes Buddy Baker, Tiny Lund, Tom Higgins, and myself. We all went fishing at Tiny's fish camp in Santee, South Carolina on a heck-uva hot day. It had to be about 100 degrees, the sun was out full force, and in South Carolina, it can get excruciatingly hot, humid, and sweaty.

"Well, Buddy decides he can't take anymore and so he says he's going to jump in the water to cool off. He's kind of goofy anyway, so he strips to his shorts, and slides over the side of the boat in the lake.

"Now Tiny didn't get his name because of his petite build—in fact, he got it because he was a tremendous man of about 230 pounds. So when Buddy goes off of one side of the boat, Tiny, on the opposite side, giggles and slides quietly off of the other side. He swims under the boat and grabs Buddy by the leg, and Lord, Buddy thinks a Carolina alligator has ahold of him. Tiny holds Buddy under, and has a grip on him that didn't feel like it was human hands on him. Buddy comes up, sputtering and spitting, and grabs the side of the boat struggling to get in.

"Just then, Tiny pops up on the opposite side, grinning. That got all over Buddy, who swore he'd kill him! Tom Higgins and I were laughing hysterically, and Tiny knew he'd gotten Buddy's goat. That was the best day—with Big Tom, Big Tiny, and Big Buddy—and they all had big hearts.

"Of all of the losses we've suffered recently, Neil Bonnett's was especially tough to deal with. Neil and I were pretty good pals, and when I worked in Talladega, we often played golf together. Neil's idea of playing golf was to hit the ball a long way. One of his golfing buddies was Hall Of Fame baseball player Virgil Trucks. Virgil and his brother lived near Birmingham, Alabama, as did Neil and the rest of the 'Alabama Gang.' We all played at least one time a week.

"Neil would call me and say, 'Hunter, can you play a round with us?' and I'd say yes. Then he'd say, 'I'm leaving my house in five minutes and I bet I can beat you to the course.' Now he was almost forty miles from the course, and I was only twenty, but I never beat him.

"I'd always accuse him of calling me from somewhere else, but I could never prove he wasn't home. That went on for awhile, until Trucks finally told me that Neil was calling from the pro shop at the golf course! I mean, I'd drive like a maniac to get there, and still lose the bet.

"Another golf story involving Neil was when we got a group together to play one day and I shared a cart with George Smith, who writes for the Anderson paper. We'd all put some beer in the carts, ride around and play.

"Well, George and I hit up, got in our cart and rolled on to the next play, noticing Neil and Trucks were laughing like crazy. George and I instinctively knew they were laughing at us. Finally we looked behind us, and George's sweater he had taken off and put in the back had caught on fire! Neil said we looked like a little steam engine! For years after that, Neil Bonnett would call us 'Steam Engine.'

"But we also had fun at the track, too. One driver, a man named Neil Castles, was absolutely terrified of snakes. So everybody put rubber snakes in his car, his truck, anywhere. He finally put out the word that who ever messed with him again would be sorry, and he put a gun in his car.

"Sure enough, the following race, there was a rubber snake in his car. So during the next caution, Neil pulled out the gun and started shooting at those he thought responsible. However, Neil neglected to tell anyone that the gun was loaded with blanks! So the other drivers were really scared. NASCAR didn't like it a bit, but what could they do?

"Helen Pearson used to say she raised four boys—her three sons, and her husband David. In fact, the reason I titled David's story I wrote, *21 Forever,* was not because he was driving the Wood Brothers car #21, but because when asked his age he'd say '21—forever!'

"I remember one time I went over to visit David, and he had two pigs he had been given that he said he wanted to fatten up for ham and bacon. He named them 'Barney,' after MRN's Bar ney Hall, and 'Jane' after Jane Hogan, the wife of Rockingham's track president, who gave the pigs to David.

"As he showed them to me, he made sure to point out that Barney was "the ugly one." But he was most disgusted at the lesson he'd learned transporting the animals from Rockingham, North Carolina to Spartanburg, South Carolina in his plane—and that was not to fly pigs in a very tight space that you were sharing with them! He said that was the worst time he ever had in the air!

"David loved to fly—and to tease me. He got a chance to do both when we were flying to Daytona one day. We were up in a big thick clouds, and David starting tapping on his radio. 'There's a problem, Jim,' he told me. 'I can't get an answer for assistance on my radio. There's only one engine on this plane, and I have no idea where we are. We could even be over the ocean!'

"Well, he had me pretty worried and anxious, and he knew it. He continued, 'Look for a hole in the clouds, and maybe we can find our way. By the way, you know I don't have any parachutes, don't you?' he teased, playing it to the hilt. Finally he pointed out a railroad track, and we followed it to Florida. He carried that off so well, that it was two years later when I was talking to someone at the Daytona airport that I finally found out. 'David sure pulled a good one on you!' they joked. But I'm just hoping that David and I have plenty of years left so that I can get even with him—if that's possible!''

*NASCAR Champion/Television Commentator/
Sports Show Host*

*Ned Jarrett has been a household name for years in the racing
world. He started his racing career in 1953 at Hickory, North
Carolina, and won the championship in 1955. After running
over six years in what is now the Busch Grand National Division, he retired from that series to find an opportunity to drive
in the now-Winston Cup Series. He is now retired altogether from
racing, but hosts one of the highest rated shows on The Nashville Network, 'Inside Winston Cup Racing,' and does commen-
tary for several other races, including ESPN's. His sons have
followed each footstep, with son Glenn a broadcaster for TNN
races, and Dale driver of the Joe Gibbs Winston Cup car.*

Ned Jarrett . . .

"I remember when I was driving for R.C. McDaniel in a '57
Chevy, and although the car was fast, it didn't last for long, so
I never was there at the finish. Well, after a Greenville, South Caro-

lina race during July 1959, I had once again broken down and did not finish the race.

"So it's Friday night and I'm riding back with my brother and a friend, and I just told them, 'I'm not doing my career a bit of good like this. I'm going to make a change.'

"Now, I'd heard that Junior Johnson had a '57 Ford for sale, and he wanted $2000 for the car. I didn't have that kind of money, but I figured that I could win that kind of money if I were to win a few races. Then I heard about two upcoming races that very weekend, one a Myrtle Beach 100 mile dirt track race, and a Charlotte, North Carolina race, both paying $950. Well, I figured in my head, if I won both of those races, I could scrape together the last $100.

"So I went to Junior's garage the next day to buy it, but I made sure I went after noon that Saturday. See, this was when banks were open on Saturday, and Junior and I both did business with the same bank. I knew if they got that check before noon it would not be any good. At that time the only thing I had was the desire.

"Right after noon, I went to Junior's shop and said, 'Junior, I believe I'll buy that race car.' Not only did I get the car, I got a real good deal, cause I bargained for the tow rig, mechanics, wheels and tires for that weekend. And guess what? I won both races! That's what launched me into Winston Cup!

"I don't believe I've ever been the kind to pull any practical jokes, but I've witnessed some of them. And I've witnessed some not so funny things, too. Like the race where Curtis Turner and Billy Myers were racing in Fayetteville, North Carolina. Turner turned into Myers and wrecked him. Billy was hopping mad!

"After the race was over, Billy grabbed a tire tool and sauntered off in pursuit of Curtis Turner. When he spotted Curtis, Myers made a bee line towards him, with that tire tool cocked up and ready. But just before he put that tool to use, Curtis turns to face him, holding a .38 pistol in his hand! 'So, Billy, what are you doing with that tire tool?' Curtis asked. Billy just gulped and said matter-of-factly, 'Just lookin' for a place to lay it down, Curtis.'

"One of the funniest stories that was related to me was from Jim Hunter, who once was with NASCAR, and is now President of the Darlington Raceway. Back when Jim was public relations director for Chrysler, David Pearson was driving a Dodge.

"Jim would go to Spartanburg, South Carolina where David lived, and they would ride to some of the races together. On one trip, where Jim was driving, Pearson, who was not known for following the speed limit when he wanted to go somewhere, kept nagging Jim and hurrying him, telling him they were late and to step on the gas.

"Well, Jim let David get to him and was soon hitting 90 mph . . . and looking in his rearview mirror, where a patrolman's blue light was pulling him over for speeding.

"When the officer came to the window, David leaned over. Taking out his handkerchief and mopping his brow he said, 'Officer, I'm so glad you pulled us! I've been trying to get him to slow down for miles!'

"Later, driving to a race again, Pearson was driving and Hunter was riding with him. Now, this is back when Chrysler had push button transmissions. So, they were sitting at a red light and a Camaro pulled up beside them with a bunch of kids in the car.

"Hunter said to Pearson, 'I believe these kids here think they can out-drag you . . . so, David, don't embarrass us, OK?' Pearson sneered and laughed at them, while Hunter was quietly slipping the car in reverse. As soon as the light turned green, Pearson stood on the gas—and demolished a pickup truck behind them. Hunter grinned at a dumbfounded Pearson and said slyly, 'That'll teach you. Next time you'll think before you tell the highway patrol you've been trying to slow me down!'

"Finally, I must relate the most memorable and largest thrill of my career, and that was at the Southern 500 in Darlington in 1965. I had set goals for myself, and one of those goals was to win this race.

"Well, Bob Colvin from Darlington came to me and asked me if I would come and speak to the Methodist Youth Fellowship before the race. I did, and while there I asked them all to pray for my safety. When I left, I went away with a peace and strong feeling of support.

"I went over to the track and plotted out our strategy with the pit crew. A gentleman walked up to me and introduced himself. He said he was from Orangeburg, South Carolina and had a strong feeling that I'd win. He said he had the same feeling in 1963 about Fireball Roberts, and he went on to win. He told me, 'My prayers are with you and I'll see you in Victory Lane.' By then, I felt just great.

"As the race wore on, I led some, then I began to overheat. Fred Lorenzen was running great, and so was Darel Dieringer. But soon, Lorenzen blew an engine, and Dieringer had my rear gear on his car.

"See, Ford had brought a special gear to the track for this race, to hopefully give us Ford drivers an edge. But at the last minute, I didn't use the gear and Bud Moore came to me and asked to borrow it for his car that Darel was driving.

"I wasn't supposed to loan it out, but I did. Well, Darel took the lead from me, and the next thing I knew, Darel was out . . . his gear burned up while leading!

"So here I keep on running, nursing an overheating car. I said my prayers and finally, when the race was over, it was my car that made it into Victory Lane. Not only that, but I won by a margin of 14 laps! That remains to this day the largest margin a NASCAR race was won. I was the last Ford in the race.

"These days, my racing enjoyment comes from watching my sons compete. But I'm sure glad they didn't have to start the way I did!"

Car Builder, Banjo's Performance

Banjo Matthews' name is synonymous with top-of-the-line race cars. When NASCAR has a technical question regarding their program, they turn to Banjo for the last word. Matthews, the premier stock car builder for NASCAR, began as a driver. He quit driving in 1963, and began building and preparing cars for winners such as Fireball Roberts ('62), Junior Johnson ('64), and Cale Yarborough ('65). In fact, Fireball Roberts was Banjo's driver when Roberts died in a fiery crash during the Charlotte 600 race. Working with drivers from Parnelli Jones to A.J. Foyt and Donnie Allison, his work is perhaps best known for the car that Michael Waltrip drove in the Bristol, Tennessee, Grand National race in 1990. As Michael hit a barrier at a high speed, his car virtually exploded, and the track became deadly silent. Looking at the car mangled on the track, many thought there was no way Waltrip could have survived such an impact. But as brother Darrell ran towards the car in a panic, his fear became relief as Michael looked up at him and winked from inside the security of the sturdy roll cage. The car had done its job and Michael raced the next day in the Winston Cup event.

Banjo Matthews . . .

"Well, I remember at Talladega, the wierdest thing happened to us. Bobby Issac was our driver, and he had just lost a good friend of his in a racing incident that very day. I believe his name was Larry Smith, and he wrecked on the very first lap.

"I was standing in the pits, checking Bobby's speed during the Talladega race, because back then, there were no spotters. I noticed that Bobby had continuously begun to lose speed and to slow down. I'd call out the times to him, and finally he came on the radio to me and said, 'Banjo, get another driver.'

"I said, 'DO WHAT?' and he said 'I'm quitting racing.' Well, I figured that the exhaust fumes were getting to him and told him to hang on, that we were getting a relief driver. I kept talking to him, trying to keep him going.

"I looked at Bud Moore, the car owner, and said, 'This fool wants to get out of the car!' Bud was flabbergasted. He said, 'Well, heck,

78

it ain't been that bad a day, and he couldn't be tired.' Bobby pulled into the pits, got out of the car, and said 'voices' told him to 'get out.' So he hops in his car and goes on home. Bobby later died in the '70's.

"There was one time that I had been interviewed for a racing magazine. It was a real good article, but I sure caused a lot of problems with the picture that went along with it. I really didn't think about how my office looked, and it was right after my heart surgery and I had other things on my mind.

"Not a week after the magazine was out, I got a call from Wayne Robinson at R.J. Reynolds, the company that sponsors the Winston Cup Series. He asked me about a particular sign on my desk, and whether I realized what it said. Well, I turn it around to see and there in big letters are the words, 'Thank You For Not Smoking.' I felt real bad about that and sent him a letter of apology 'from the bottom of my bypassed heart.'

"Then, if that wasn't enough, I got a call from the folks at Ford Motor Company, whom I was working with at the time. Know what else was in the picture? A big ol' Chevrolet emblem!"

DOUG SKEEN

Engine Builder

Doug Skeen has been in NASCAR racing "off and on for about thirty years." In 1963, Doug and a friend bought a Grand National car from Buck Baker for $3000. It was a '61 Pontiac with a spare motor, and it just happened to be the same car that Wendell Scott, the first black racer, won his only race in at Jacksonville. They took it home to Jefferson City, Tennessee, painted it, and assigned crew jobs to the members. Doug chose to be jackman, "cause it seemed the job where I could least likely screw up." Doug soon realized how expensive being a car owner was, and found his racing home building engines. Presently, he is a representative for AutoLite Spark Plugs.

Doug Skeen . . .

"Have you ever met anyone who when asked to talk is at a loss for words? I guess I'll start with when I began my illustrious career as a jackman. I chose jacking cause I figured there was no way I could screw up doing that. Well, I was wrong.

"That was the days before the aluminum jacks; the jack weighed about 135 pounds, but unfortunately, so did I! It was just an old floor jack out of the garage. So on the first pit stop, I could barely get around with that big ol' jack to lift the car up.

"Well, the right front tire changer gets the wheel off and the new one on, and a lug nut rolls under the right front wheel. And just as I let the jack down and unscrewed the handle, he puts his hand down there to brush the lug nut away! I had let the car down on his hand!

"So here he is standing up, bending over with his hand under the right front tire, and me with the jack out! So I put the jack back underneath, and jack the car back up. The best thing is that none of this hurt him, because oddly enough, his two fingers under the tire were on each side of the lug nut, and the nut was what kept the tire from crushing his hand! That was our worst pit stop, but I guarantee you there were plenty more that were almost as bad.

"This story happened only recently, but it still tickles me. This one is about Busch Grand National champion, Tommy Ellis. If you know Tommy, you can appreciate this, but if not, Tommy was short-fused to say the least.

"A couple of years ago, we were at Rockingham. Tommy was there with his race car, with only one engine. So during the last practice session, he blows his motor up. Since we were good friends, and I had worked with him before, he puts the task on me to please borrow an engine, cause he figured nobody would lend him one if he asked . . . and he probably was right. Well, the first person I go to is Jeff Hensley, since he had a spare engine that I had built.

"I said 'Jeff, would you consider loaning Tommy this motor?' Jeff said, kind of reluctantly, 'Yeah, yeah, ok . . . for you.' I asked how much and he said it wouldn't cost anything, just borrow it and if something happens to it, that's it.

"Well, we got it in Tommy's car, barely made the race, I mean just barely. After fifteen or twenty laps into the event, I could see it starting to burn a piston, a little smoke . . . then a little more smoke, and finally the thing exploded.

"So here comes Tommy drifting into the infield, jumps out of the car and goes to sit and sulk in this captain's chair. You can tell he's in one of his moods—he's mad, he looks like he's going to explode. So I knew not to say anything to him, and I kept my distance and stayed up on the top of the truck and just watched him.

"Finally he started getting calmed down, so I got down off of the truck to talk to him. I said, 'Tommy, looks like you had a little bit of bad luck, didn't you?' And he wouldn't say anything.

"I said, 'What happened?' He just scowled and said, 'Your old motor blowed up!' Then he said, 'Thanks a lot! If you hadn't of gotten them to loan me that old motor, I'd be halfway home by now!'

"Another Tommy Ellis story—he's got this friend named Chuck. And Chuck never comes to the races unless Tommy is there. Chuck's his buddy, and to him, whatever Tommy says is OK.

"In Rougemont, a couple of years ago, Chuck was there, and Tommy was having a terrible time getting the car set up. He tried everything and for the life of him couldn't get it to handle. It got to where he just got so exasperated he comes in, jumps out of the car, and stands over near me and Chuck. He starts talking to neither one of us, and yet both of us, too, and says, 'I don't know what to do. I just don't know what else I can do. I've tried everything, I've changed every spring, I just . . . I just don't know what to do!'

"And Chuck says, 'Tommy, why don't you . . .' Then Tommy says, 'Shut up, Chuck! I know what I'm doing!'

"I did a lot of work with Tommy, and I guess that's why most of my stories are about Tommy. I like Tommy—Tommy's a good racer, and I wish he would hurry and come back. When we raced at Richmond, I sent him word that even if he never raced again, to please just show up so we could see him. I said that things had gotten much too quiet, that we hadn't had a controversy all weekend!

"Right before Tommy stopped racing, I remember we were in Louden, New Hampshire. Tommy had really been running well, and they were out practicing the cars, when Tommy wrecked his car. Tommy comes in fuming . . . he looked like if you put a pin in him, he would pop. He's sitting, slumped down in his chair, and his wife Brenda was rubbing his shoulders. I come over and say, 'Tommy, buddy, what happened out there?'

" 'It's all that Troy Bebe's fault!' he screamed. 'He was driving right in the place I needed to spin to!'

"Back in the days before the Charlotte Speedway, I was at a little diner one night eating supper, the day before the Darlington race. Curtis Turner was in there trying to sell shares in this speedway that he was gonna build in Charlotte.

"Nobody seemed very interested in it. In fact, I didn't see him sell any. I didn't have any money to buy any, and probably wouldn't have if I did. See, if you knew Curtis Turner, you'd think it was another one of his pipe dreams that would never get off the ground.

"But the stocks that he was selling at the time turned into the Charlotte Motor Speedway. If you could have looked into the future a good ways, it would have been a great deal. I still have an old proposal that he left me, and I don't remember how much the stock went for, but it would be a fabulous investment today!"

HUMPY WHEELER

Promoter

Humpy Wheeler began his career in racing operating dirt tracks from 1960 until 1963, when he moved to the Firestone Tire Company. He continued with Firestone until 1970, when he got out of racing for five years. But a few visits to the dirt tracks in those years was just not enough and he decided to make the move to the big time . . . really BIG time, where he began with the Charlotte Motor Speedway. Today, Wheeler has made the CMS into the most famous NASCAR track in America, and is currently President and General Manager.

Humpy Wheeler . . .

"Back in 1961, I was operating a dirt track in Gastonia, North Carolina, called the Robinwood Speedway. I was every bit of 21 years old then, I guess, and I thought I knew something about racing. So what I thought would really bring in larger crowds would be attracting more women to the races.

"Now the women's restroom at the Robinwood Speedway—

which was a real high banked dirt track—was not anything any-one, including a man, would want to go to. So I got this great idea to build a new restroom. Unfortunately, I built it off the fourth turn. On the second night the restroom was functional, a car went out of control, went over the wall, and landed right on top of the women's restroom!

"But the real problem was . . . there was someone in it! It was a lady around 35 years old, and she really was not hurt very badly. She didn't break anything, but she was bruised and scratched some. We took her to the hospital and they later released her.

"Well, about six weeks later, I got hit with a $100,000 lawsuit! So during the 'discovery' part of the trial—that's where my law-yer questioned her about the incident—I'm sitting in there with my lawyer and this lady walks in. She's fairly attractive, and quite well dressed for the kind of women that went to the dirt tracks back in those days. Then, my lawyer begins cross-examining her about her name, address, and so on; and suddenly he did an abso-lute brilliant thing.

"He said, 'What were you doing in the restroom?' She got all huffy and said, 'That's none of your business!' The attorney said,

'That's all my business, and that's what I'm going to ask you on the witness stand!'

"Well, that just completely unglued her! She didn't want to get on that witness stand and talk about what she was doing in the restroom! We settled the case the next day for $5000!

"We had a particular pre-race show here at Charlotte Motor Speedway one time, and as everyone knows, we like to do our pre-race shows up big. Now, Memorial Day is pretty much patriotic, but during the October events is when we do the 'goofy' stuff.

"We were sitting here one day in the summertime thinking about what we were going to do for the October show and we got the Guiness Book of World Records people out to get some ideas of what to do—like the world's largest sandwich or whatever. We find out that the largest band ever put together was 4500 people. So we decided in October we'd beat that. We went to work, and ended up with 5200 marchers. We got every high school and college marching band we could find within 150 miles from here.

"You know, when you run a place like this you have to think of every little repercussion. However, we forgot about one particular repercussion, but it was October, so it didn't cross our minds. October is usually cool, but the day of the race it was 85 degrees in the morning!

"Now, it was to be 2600 band members coming in the back gate, and march around to the front, and 2600 on the front side march around the other way and meet in the middle on the grass area. Well, the wind stopped blowing, and the temperature on the roof was 85, so it had to be 90 down there on the asphalt.

"Suddenly, about six of the band members collapsed. Jay Howard, who was the guy who actually put the show together here, was standing next to me on the top of the tower like we always do when the pre-race shows start. We thought the fainting was just an isolated incident, but when the bands started playing, eight more went down in about two minutes!

"Then Jay says, 'Humpy, we've got a real problem here!' And while he said that, another eight fell down! I looked at him, shrugged, and said, 'Jay, the show goes on!' Within seconds of saying that, about forty hit the ground! I turned to Jay and said, 'Jay . . . the show's been canceled!'

"We ended up treating over seventy of them in the hospital for dehydration. This incident was not funny for about a year!

"One of the things that people in racing do that they don't talk about is what they talk about to each other going to the track, whether they're in a plane or a car.

"Well, Little Bud Moore, who was a great short track driver just getting into Winston Cup racing, Buddy Baker, and I were driving to Daytona. We always drove at night because you could make it in about six hours if the cops weren't out. This was before we all had airplanes, sometime in the '60's.

"After about an hour of riding, we had run out of racing things to talk about, and of course Buddy was driving because he wouldn't let anyone else drive. So I'm sitting in the back seat, and Bud and Buddy were in the front. They both were both pilots at the time, and somehow, we got to talking about flying saucers.

"Bud said, 'Well, I don't believe in flying saucers. It's just an optical illusion.' I told them that there was an awful lot of scientific evidence about UFO's, and I went into this big dissertation of what I knew about them. That wasn't a whole lot, but it was more than some people.

"Well, Buddy was just quietly driving along at about 90 mph, and Bud and I got into an argument about the reality of flying saucers. And it got to the point where it almost came to blows. I was saying there are, and Bud was saying there was no way, it was all lights, illusions, and the airport doing strange things. Finally he said, really loud, 'If there were flying saucers, they would have contacted us already!'

"Buddy finally speaks up after all this time and asks, 'How could you talk to an ant?' That just stopped the conversation, and nobody said anything for a long time after that!

"We were having trouble selling tickets here at CMS in 1976 for the 600. Janet Guthrie was trying to be the first woman to run a major race in the United States, and she was trying that same weekend for the Indy 500. So even the Charlotte Observer paper was playing the Indianapolis race up more than the 600, that's how bad it got.

"It was the last day of qualifying at Indy. I worked up there for awhile, so I'm pretty good at finding people for what I need. So I start talking to a couple of the crew chiefs up there and they said Janet wouldn't make the field, because she just didn't have the car for it. Then I tried to talk to her, but she didn't want to talk to me; I guess I represented failure.

"Well, she missed making the field by about a mile or two per hour. I waited about thirty minutes before I called her in the garage. I had all these tickets left to sell, so I said, 'Janet, I'd like to get you down here to run in the 600. This, in my opinion, would be a greater feat for a woman than running Indy because those cars are not that physically demanding to drive like a stock car, and the race is a hundred miles longer.'

"She said: 'If I can have A.J. Foyt's stock car that he put on the pole and a really top-notch crew chief, I'll come.' So we flew up there and got her, and we didn't even have to call a press conference because the press followed us back to Charlotte. Press even met us at the airport . . . I mean, it was all over the place about Janet.

"We bought Foyt's car that he had in Daytona, and we got Ralph Moody to be the crew chief. We already had a sponsor—NAPA—

and she made the race. We sold out of tickets the next day, the most we'd ever sold in one day, and CMS became the focal point of racing. For the first time, Charlotte overwhelmed Indy!

"When you're a track operator, a lot of strange things run through your mind on race day. Like, what would happen if the lead car spins in front of the whole field and you have 600 miles to go, but thirty of the cars have been taken out? It's never happened before, but you think about it. (We did have a twenty car pileup here one time at the start of the race!)

"So you're trying to think of every single thing that could happen that probably won't, but when it does you'll be prepared for it.

"Well, halfway through the race, Janet's still in it, and she's running pretty well. She's in about 20th place, and when you see that flag at the halfway mark, every track operator in the world sighs this big sigh of relief. All you have to do is make one more lap and it can rain, snow, whatever, and the race can end. So I'm up there in the tower watching this, and I'm feeling great.

"Then my brother David, who keeps me in line and keeps my

humility at its proper level, comes up to the control tower and he whacks me in the back like he does when there's a problem. He says, 'Buster, you got BIG problems!'

"I said, 'What do you mean? The race is past halfway!' He said, 'You're sucking air.'

"Now, that is the worst possible thing I could have heard, because we had a big array of wells around the track. This is before we got city water. At that time we used about 350,000 gallons of water per race. When he said 'sucking air,' it meant there was no water left in those storage tanks . . . we were out of water!

"I simply cannot tell you. There are hardly any worse crises that could exist than a track being out of water—because pretty much the business we're in here is not only racing . . . it's racing and toilets!

"'So I say, 'Oh, my Lord . . .' We had to immediately get on the phone. I could not imagine what happened . . . we had more than enough water prepared. So I was calling, everyone on my staff was calling different volunteer fire departments, getting every one we could within fifty miles of Charlotte. The conversation would go something like this.

95

"The volunteer fire department would answer the phone, I'd tell them, 'Hello, this is Humpy Wheeler, do you have a tank truck?' 'Yea.' 'How many gallons of water do you have available?' 'Oh, about 2000.' 'Can you bring it to the speedway and get here in thirty minutes? We'll donate $500 to you.'

"And every one of them did it, cause $500 in 1976 for a volunteer fire department was pretty good. I guess folks thought there was a disaster at CMS, because we had about forty five trucks running in here, red lights blaring, everybody getting out of their way, Memorial Day weekend, and people got all excited.

"Now, the interesting question was: Why did we run out of water? We ran out of water because so many females showed up! See, this was back in the days when only 15% of the crowd were women. We figured we sold a couple of thousand tickets to the race to just one person, which was real strange because it never happened before or since. I mean, very few people call up saying they want one ticket. Usually it's a pair.

"Well, what happened was it was women that wanted to come out here and see Janet run, and the husband or boyfriend didn't. So we had about 35% of the crowd being women. We found out

96

later that we had run out of toilet paper thirty minutes before the water was gone! Now fortunately, we did have a truckload of it here, and we were able to get it into the restrooms. That wasn't funny then, but I can say that it is funny now!

"Bobby Isaac and I used to go a lot of places together. This was when he was racing. Well, one time, we went to Bristol together. This was in the late '60's, and as now, Bristol did not have a tunnel. We went up in my car, and we had to share motel rooms cause money was scarce in those days. It was also during the times that nobody would steal a car at a racetrack.

"Well, 5 p.m. came and practice was over. I was going back to my car and looking around, but it wasn't there. I thought, 'Where in the heck is my car?' It was a Dodge 500, a limited edition Dodge, and only five hundred of them were made. So it was very valuable, and I had this car on loan from Chrysler under the condition if I lost it I would have to pay them what it was worth, which was a fortune to me.

"I distinctly remembered parking the car in the infield, at the second turn . . . and it wasn't there. Bobby said, 'You walk one way and I'll go the other way.' And we still couldn't find the car. By that time, people started leaving, cause the garage was closed. An hour later, there's not a car in the infield!

"I said, 'Oh my Lord, how can anybody steal this car, because nobody could get out of the infield!' There was no tunnel! So I told Bobby, 'Let's go find the police to report a stolen car.' Well, we walked outside the track down to NASCAR registration. The highway patrol station was about a hundred feet away.

"I told the NASCAR official that was there that day the whole story. I didn't even know what the license was! After telling him the story, I was walking toward the highway patrol station when the NASCAR official yelled behind me, 'Hey, wait a minute! We've found your car.'

"It was hidden behind the NASCAR registration trailer. Now, there was only one person that could have pulled this on me, and he never would admit it. I always used to put my keys on the top of the left rear tire, and left it locked so nobody could steal anything.

"But how that car got from the infield to NASCAR registration— across the track—I absolutely guarantee you that Bobby Isaac did that!

"I kept him up till 1 a.m. trying to get him to admit it, but he wouldn't. And the worst part is to this very day, I still have no idea how it happened. Bobby never admitted it! See, he was a real quiet type of a person, but he'd pull stunts like this once and awhile just to liven things up. I truly feel he did it.

"I have a Rolex watch that I love dearly. On the back is inscribed 'Winners never quit—Quitters never win.' And in the middle it says 'Talladega 500.'

"In '69, when Talladega was built, all the factory drivers boycotted the first race. The track was too fast, and their tires were torn all to pieces, they said. Bobby Isaac was the only factory driver that stayed to run in the race. So Bill France, Sr. gave him this watch for doing that.

"Later, as Banjo Matthews remembered, Bobby said that voices, or God, told him to get out of the race car while he was racing at Talladega. He had lost a good friend in a wreck there, and Talladega was a bad omen for him. So he decided to get rid of all remembrances of Talladega, Alabama. Anything that remotely reminded of that place was gone. He essentially quit Winston Cup racing, and went to racing at Hickory, North Carolina. That was where he got his first start.

"Bobby knew that I liked Rolex watches. So he came to see me one day and said, 'You've always liked this watch, haven't you? I've never even worn it . . . never put it on. Well, I want you to buy this watch from me.'

"I said, 'Naw, I'm not going to do that Bobby, that watch is a special gift to you.' He argued with me. No, no, he didn't want it, didn't want anything with Talladega on it. He told me he didn't want it back, and for me to think about it. Then he walked around my desk and dropped it into my drawer. He said 'Just pay me in a couple of weeks.' I kept telling him I couldn't possibly buy this watch, that it was like buying a trophy from somebody.

"Well, a week later, Tom Pistone called me up. He said, 'I need to come by and get a check from you, Humpy.' I said 'A check? What are you talking about?'

"Tom said, 'Well, I just got through fixing Bobby Isaac's race car, and he said you owed him the same amount of money that I'm charging him for this Hickory car to be fixed!"

WADDELL WILSON

Crew Chief

Waddell Wilson's name has become synonymous with success. He began his career studying at the Nashville Diesel College in 1963. He later found himself in motorsports working for the legendary Holman-Moody Racing organization, building engines for names such as Fireball Roberts, Fred Lorenzen, A.J. Foyt, and David Pearson. In time, his reputation grew and he later served as crew chief for Buddy Baker, Bobby Allison, Cale Yarborough, Al Unser Jr., Geoff Bodine, and Ricky Rudd. He won two championships with Benny Parsons and David Pearson; he also won five Daytona 500 races in a row, winning the '84 qualifying race (the Twin 125) and the '84 500 from the pole position! With over 20 years NASCAR history, Waddell reminisces fondly his career memories.

Waddell Wilson . . .

"It seems that we in the NASCAR community have relied on

the dime store rubber snake to relieve tension and boredom since racing began. Some of my favorite memories revolve around that aggravating piece of plastic.

"In or around 1989, we were in Pocono. At that track, there are a lot of fans in the infield that like to congregate around the garage area fence, where we park our haulers, to get a glimpse of their favorite driver.

"In the hauler was a microwave oven, and inside this microwave I had put some lunch to warm up. However, when I reached inside, I didn't get my lunch. Instead, someone had planted a rubber snake!

"When I pulled it out of the oven, it aggravated me so bad that I just took the thing and threw it over my head as far as I could sling it—and wouldn't you know the snake landed in the middle of a huge crowd outside the fence! You should have seen those people scatter, running and falling all over each other. By the time I got to them two fellas had cut the harmless lil' rubber snake to a million pieces!

"You know, most of the sportswriters we deal with are pretty decent. Oh, sometimes we get put out with them when they stick a microphone or camera in your face while you're about to lose your temper, but we let it roll off our back and then get even with them in a harmless kind of way.

"One time there was this female reporter that we thought would be fun to play with. We were in Atlanta, and we kept this small box around to pull this trick with. We would tell folks that in this box was a mongoose, a very small animal that was supposed to be really vicious.

"This lady reporter was quite enthused about seeing a mongoose in this box, while what was really inside was only a string attached to a furry tail. The more we'd talk about this mongoose, the more she wanted to get a look at it. We told her to be real careful, and she approached the box very slowly, and kept saying, 'I can't see it . . . I can't see it.'

"Right as she got up to where her face was inches from the box, we pulled on the toy tail and jerked it in her face! Well, most people kind of scream or yell and jump back—but not this lady. She just stood there, looking at us with no expression on her face . . .

and commenced to wet all over herself! At that time, NASCAR confiscated the box and put a stop to that joke!

"Now, that Henry Benfield . . . he's supplied me with a lot of laughs. Henry is the truck driver for Junior Johnson, and there isn't anyone in that garage area that can pull a stunt like him.

"We were in Phoenix in '91, and since Henry always has a rubber snake with him, he thought he'd pass the time by messin' with those boys from the #15 car of Bud Moore. It seems one of those guys, Harold, has a snake phobia.

"Henry started early that Saturday morning, telling Harold to be careful and watch out, because that particular desert racetrack had rattlesnakes everywhere. He would sneak up behind Harold every so often and hiss like a snake, 'till it got to the point where poor Harold was a nervous wreck. Then, in the middle of the afternoon, when the Winston West Division was running their race, Henry watched his pal Harold go up into the grandstands to watch the feature, and maybe to get away from Henry some, too.

"Well, Henry started grinning to himself and followed Harold. He saw where Harold was sitting, and crawled underneath the grandstands right under where Harold was seated. Then he took a rubber snake out of his pocket, carefully wrapped it around Harold's ankle, hissed loud and pinched Harold on the bottom of his leg.

"Harold's head jerked down to look and he screamed so loud you could hear that yell above the sound of 40 race engines! Harold took off, clearing out the next three rows of fans sitting in front of him, tripping over people and shoving them out of his way! Last I saw of Henry that day, he was holding his side laughing so hard he couldn't get his breath!

"These days there doesn't seem time to fool around as much 'cause you have to concentrate on keeping your sponsors happy, trying to keep ahead of your competitors, and ensuring the work gets done on the car.

"Sometimes there'll be an occasional prank, like maybe having a nasty smell in your hotel room because someone got a fish at the market and put it in your bed that morning. By the time you get back in the evening, you can hardly get a breath 'cause the smell is so rotten.

"Sometimes the pranks aren't even good ones. I remember when I was with Bobby Allison. He was the championship points leader, and we were at the Texas World Speedway. He came in for his first pit stop, so we of course tried to gas up. But the car wouldn't take the fuel. We changed the tires, and put in as much gas as possible, getting him out before the pace car.

"He came in once more, so as not to get a lap down, and again, the car wouldn't take the gas. We jerked the vent hose off and lo, someone had stuck a rag in it. But I want to emphasize that those incidents are very isolated.

"As competitive as it is out there, I can't think of anyone that wouldn't help you if you needed it. Competing crew members help out another crew when an air wrench breaks in the middle of a pit stop, a car needs a shove, or a part needs to be borrowed.

"Like I was saying, it's a bit more serious now, but there was one driver I remember that if he were alive today, he would give the most patient of car owners a case of bad nerves and a head of gray hair. That driver was Curtis Turner.

"We were in Richmond one hot Sunday afternoon. Ol' Curtis fell out of the race a bit early, and he was not too happy about ending his day prematurely. We had always called Curtis the 'Wild One,' and by the time he left the track, he not only was wild, he was in a foul mood.

"Curtis headed to collect his things at the Holiday Inn, where his room was on the ground level. He was ready to get the heck out of Dodge, and too aggravated to check out like any normal person. So he backed his vehicle up to the plate glass window of his room, rammed right through it, and proceeded to get his bags and head home.

"Heck, one night in Charlotte, he was driving along and some man with his car headlights on high beam was behind Curtis at the red light. The lights were blinding Curtis, so he simply put his car in reverse and plowed into the front end of that car to dim the lights for that car. Served the purpose . . . his lights weren't too bright then!

"Joe Weatherly was another one. He was wild and liked to party, too. Curtis told me about one night while he and Joe were in Daytona. Back then, they raced on the beach, and drove their cars back and forth to the hotel.

"Well, on this particular night, those two were driving down highway A1A, to the hotel. Up ahead a mile or so was a strange curve in the road, where you had to make a 90 degree turn to the left, and then immediately a 90 degree turn to the right. Curtis was driving his car, and Joe said, 'Curtis, I'll bet a good driver like you can make those turns going 90 mph.'

"Turner said, 'No way!' Well, Joe kept on pushing so Curtis had to take the challenge. He hits 90 mph, takes the first turn then immediately slammed his race car/street car into the side of a motel! Joe looked over at a fuming Curtis, who had just ruined his ride, and says, 'Well, I guess you were right—you really couldn't take that turn!'"

CALE YARBOROUGH

Stock Car Driver/Owner

Cale Yarborough began his 'checkered' career in the sleepy little town of Sardis, South Carolina, where his very first race was in the Soap Box Derby. He lost the race, but did not lose the desire to race and to win. He started with local dirt tracks, and finished with a Winston Cup Championship, and world recognition as a legendary NASCAR driver. Today, a retired Cale owns Cale Yarborough Motorsports, fielding a stock car of his own.

Cale Yarborough . . .

"I remember dust being a problem at the Columbia Speedway in South Carolina. It got so dusty at times that you couldn't see a thing. All you could do was follow the guy in front of you and hope that he knew what he was doing, or at least see where he was going. To this day, I still have some eye problems, with my eyes burning. I'm sure it's from all that dust I used to run in.

"One night it was so bad at Columbia, that I was following this car in front of me. I couldn't understand why. He kept getting slower and slower and I got slower and slower behind him. I figured it must be a lot of traffic, or that someone had spun ahead.

"Finally, he completely stopped, and I ran into him. I got out of the car and started to walk up to him and ask him what the heck he was doing. The dust had settled a little by then, and I could see where we were. In all that dust, I followed that car right into the pits!

"There's one funny thing that sticks in my mind about a Nashville, Tennessee, race. In the driver's meeting, we were told to hold it down on the pace lap; they always told us that, but nobody listened.

"Buck Baker piped up: 'Yea, we know . . . don't knock the clown down until they drop the green.' He was referring to the big billboard with the clown in the middle of it outside the fence at turn three. I forgot what it was advertising.

"They hadn't anymore dropped the green flag when Buck went flying into turn three and blew a tire. His race car sailed over the fence, and I swear that it went straight through the clown's mouth!

I saw it happen, and I laughed so hard that I nearly wrecked. After the race Buck laughed about it too, saying, 'Well, you have to admit, my aim sure was good!'

"After the races, we'd always go to this roadhouse and some of the guys would let off some steam and get noisy. Somehow a fight always happened.

"Lee Roy Yarbrough was the worst about starting fights. He couldn't go to the men's room without taking a swing at someone. I never understood it. He couldn't fight at all, but that never stopped him. He would punch some guy and then end up on the short end of the stick, getting pulverized every time.

"Tiny Lund, a tremendous man who stood 6'5" and weighed 260 pounds, was a driver in our group, and he always ended up finishing the fight for Lee Roy. It was the same every time. Lee Roy would start it and Tiny would end it. But Tiny was so big and tough, that if you did hit him, he'd just laugh. You just couldn't hurt him.

"Bubba Into was another one of our group that was tough. He wasn't as big as Tiny, but he was tough and as mean as he'd wanna

111

be if you got him mad. The biggest mistake Lee Roy ever made was the night he got into a fight with Bubba.

"It wasn't the argument itself that was the mistake; we argued all the time. But Lee Roy got mad that night. He grabbed a Coke bottle and hit Bubba over the head with it, so hard that it broke the bottle, and you know how thick those old Coke bottles were. It was like hitting someone with a lead pipe.

"Bubba stood there with a look of amazement on his face. He didn't even blink. He just looked at Lee Roy and said in a soft easy drawl, 'You really shouldn't have done that, Lee Roy.' I said to myself, 'Oh, Lord,' and Lee Roy knew at that moment that he had done something real bad.

"Bubba picked up Lee Roy and threw him through a window—a closed window, that is. We all grabbed Bubba and calmed him down, cause he was ready to go after Lee Roy. He may have even killed him. But in a few minutes Lee Roy peeked through the front door and said, 'Listen, Bubba . . . I'm, uh, well . . . I'm sorry 'bout the Coke bottle.'

"Bubba looked around and said, 'Aw, that's O.K., Lee Roy . . .

You can pay for the window.' 'Sure Bubba!' Lee Roy said. 'Now, uh, can you help me pick the glass out of my hair?'

"I heard this particular story once about Curtis Turner and his airplane. He and a friend were flying over Gaffney, South Carolina, when they ran out of booze. That's right, booze. Curtis didn't think a thing about flying and drinking.

" 'No problem,' Curtis said. 'I've got a friend down there in Gaffney who runs a bootleg business, so we'll just land this rascal on the highway and then take right off. Nobody'll ever see us.'

"Well, that sounded good to his buddy. After all, it was Saturday, and outside of the city limits, so why not? The only problem was that there was a Little League game just letting out when Curtis was about to touch down on the highway in his twin-engine Aero-Commander. There was traffic coming at him, so he pulled back on the stick and decided to get out of there. He was scared to death someone had gotten his plane number and reported him to the FAA.

"Curtis flew all the way back to Charlotte at about fifty feet off the ground so they wouldn't pick him up on the radar. When he got back, he decided to land in Concord, North Carolina, a few miles northeast of Charlotte. He chose that airport because they didn't have a radar. In fact, they only had a small shack and a man who answered radio calls.

"As Curtis went in he said, 'This is murghp-humpf-tprumghf, requesting permission to land,' purposely garbling his number so it wouldn't be picked up anywhere else on the radar.

"The voice at the shack of the Concord landing strip radioed in, 'It's no use Curtis, they're looking for you all over the South!' The incident cost Curtis his flying license, but didn't stop him from flying. Said he could never find the license, anyway!

"Little Joe Weatherly was always called the Clown Prince of Racing, so he tried hard to live up to it. He and Curtis Turner borrowed the Darlington pace car one night and ended up in a contest to see which one could drive closest to the telephone poles. The closer Curtis got, the more Joe was aggravated. 'You call that close?' he would say. So Curtis got closer. Far too close most of the time. When Joe took over, it was the same thing.

"When they brought the car back, Darlington track general

manager Bob Colvin (who lent them the car in a weak moment) stopped pacing the floor to look out his office window at the pace car. They had parked it with the left side facing his office. 'Wow', he said, 'I'm sure glad to see it in one piece. I have to tell you boys, I thought y'all might tear it up!' Curtis said, 'Aw, Bob we wouldn't do that . . . it's the pace car!'

"It wasn't until Bob got in the car that night that he noticed the broken glass in the right window. He got out and ran around the car. The whole right side of the car was gone . . . the side the grandstands see!

"Lil' Joe always had some practical joke to play on people. That year at Darlington, he tossed a rubber snake into everybody's car just as they were ready to pull out of the pits to practice. Some came right out of their cars, and Joe laughed like mad.

"He did it to me. I didn't leave the car, but it did scare me. When I went home that night, I went snake hunting and sure enough, I found a five-foot-long rattlesnake. I got the forked stick on his head and caught it, then took it home and pulled out his fangs with a pair of pliers. Now, that's something you have to be pretty careful about doing! I put the snake in a burlap bag, and took it to the track with me the next day.

"I was in luck. Joe was in his race car. I went up to his car, and tossed it right into his lap. He looked at it, and then up at me with an 'are-you-kidding?' look on his face. Then, the snake started to rattle.

"Joe froze. Then he let out a war whoop, and I've never seen anyone get a seat belt off and get out of a car so fast! He was white as a ghost! But as soon as he stopped shaking, he turned red. You could see him reaching the boiling point. Everybody was falling on the ground laughing. Joe ran to his toolbox, got out a ball peen hammer, and took off after me. I was running like never before, because I knew he would kill me if he caught me! You know, I don't think he ever touched a rubber snake again, much less brought another one to the track!

"Junior Johnson was a great stock car driver, and one of the best car builders to ever hit NASCAR. He is also a very colorful man. In fact, he was so good that the late Bill France, Sr., went to Junior after one of the races and said, 'Junior, you're really doing well. In fact, you're doing so well that we expect you to drive all thirty races on the schedule this year.'

"Junior replied, 'Naw, Bill, I'm only gonna run a few of them, just to see if I like it or not.' Bill retorted, 'But you're committed, Junior.'

" 'Naw, Bill . . . what it is, is I'm involved,' comes back Junior. Then Bill gets a little stern with Junior and says 'No, you're committed!'

"So Junior looks at him a minute and then says, 'Bill, you got the words all wrong. Now listen: if you sit down to a breakfast tomorrow of bacon and eggs, the chicken is involved. The pig is committed!'

"Junior ran all the races he wanted to."

HOW TO ORDER THIS BOOK

If your local bookstore or souvenir shop is out of *STOCK CAR LEGENDS: The Laughs, Practical Jokes, and Fun Stories, From Racing's Greats* and you'd like to have a couple of extra copies for the guys in the pit, you can order directly from the publisher by sending a check or money order for $6.95 per book plus $2.00 for shipping and handling. Mail to:

Stock Car Legends
PREMIUM PRESS AMERICA
P.O. Box 159015
Nashville, TN 37215-9015
1-800-891-7323

Allow 2-4 weeks for delivery.

Other Stock Car books from Premium Press America:
The Great American Stock Car Racing Trivia Book
Stock Car Drivers and Tracks
Stock Car For Kids